HOW IT HAPPENED

HOW IT HAPPENED

The 2016
Presidential Campaign
in Jest and Verse

Dear Susan,
Hope you enjoy
this book.

Erika S. Fine   *Erika*

POET PUNDIT PRESS

BROOKLINE, MASSACHUSETTS

ISBN 13: 978-0-692-05402-4
Library of Congress Control Number: 2018930318
Printed in the United States of America
First Printing: 2018
22 21 20 19 18   5 4 3 2 1

Book design by Ryan Scheife, Mayfly Design

Poet Pundit Press
Brookline, MA
www.poetpunditpress.com

In memory of my father, Harold J. Fine, who entertained me with amusing poems when I was a child, and my maternal grandfather, Samuel M. Honig, who wrote poems for family, friends, and a local newsweekly.

CONTENTS

AUTHOR'S NOTE

The Best and Worst in Jest and Verse

No one could have foreseen the tumult and tawdriness of the 2015–16 presidential election campaign. Writing light verse helped me manage the highs and lows with equanimity.

Ironically, I wrote my first poem of the season on November 8, 2015, exactly one year before the startling election of November 8, 2016. I had no idea that poem would be the first of many.

I wrote the poems while the news they covered was still fresh. They lampoon all the candidates, but not equally: if you are a Trump fan, this book is probably not for you.

Trump's inauguration was four days after I composed the final poem in this book. Since then, following the news has become a breathless venture, and I have struggled to find a balance between escapism and obsession. I also took a break from writing poems, but I hope to return to "poet punditry" soon.

PART ONE

Primary Season

November 2015

A Year to Go

The 2015–16 presidential primary season was a brazen spectacle. The Republicans started out with 17 candidates. As the son and brother of U.S. presidents, former Florida Governor Jeb Bush was considered the favorite.

The Democrats opened the season with six candidates, and three dropped out early on. Hillary Clinton was expected to enjoy a smooth ride to the nomination. As a former First Lady, two-term Senator, and recent Secretary of State, she had a strong financial network and support base.

The predictions, however, were wrong.

• • •

By the beginning of November 2015, eight candidates were eligible to participate in the Republican's upcoming primetime debate, based on their scores in national polls:

- Former Florida Governor **Jeb Bush**
- Retired neurosurgeon **Ben Carson**
- Texas Senator **Ted Cruz**
- Business executive **Carly Fiorina**
- Ohio Governor **John Kasich**
- Kentucky Senator **Rand Paul**
- Florida Senator **Marco Rubio**
- Real-estate-magnate-cum-TV-showman **Donald Trump**

On the Democratic side, former Secretary of State **Hillary Clinton**, Vermont Senator **Bernie Sanders**, and former Maryland Governor **Martin O'Malley** qualified to participate in their party's November debate.

Election Selection

November 8, 2015

Carson, you can slice a brain
But somehow you cannot explain
Your skepticism toward vaccines
And doubts about your wayward teens.

Rubio, your spending woes
Are catnip to your jealous foes.
But still, your brash and youthful charm
Has put the Bush team on alarm.

Jeb, we thought you'd be the heir,
Not bullied by a billionaire.
Are you as hapless as you seem
While limping toward your parents' dream?

Trump, your xenophobic glee,
And paucity on policy,
And joy at playing bottom feeder
Combine to show you're not a leader.

Carly, you told many lies
About your brilliant business rise
But never did you tell the tale
Of letting Hewlett Packard fail.

Bernie, you're surprising all—
We thought by now you'd surely stall,
Yet your campaign is strong and deft,
A coup for someone so far left.

Hillary, you lead the pack
Though earnest Bernie's not far back
He's consistent, frank, sincere,
While your positions sway and veer.

Poor ***O'Malley***, you lean left
But your campaign won't pick up heft
Yet voters now are keeping tabs
On who has got the firmest abs.

So ... watch the candidates debate!
Will they lie or play it straight?
Will they duck or take the bait?
Are they fit for head of state?

▶ The week of November 8, 2015, was the first time the two parties held debates within a close time frame—the Republicans on November 10 and the Democrats on November 14. Controversy and criticism abounded in anticipation of the two showdowns. For example:

- Even though **Carson**, a man of science, acknowledged that vaccines don't cause autism, he seemed to support making vaccination optional, a formerly fringe idea that had entered the Republican mainstream. Carson's personal credibility was also questionable. He claimed that as a young teen, he had pulled a knife on a friend, but details of his account changed over time. Investigative journalists could not find anyone who could verify the story, leading some to suggest that Carson had fabricated it to exaggerate his journey from poverty to Yale to brain surgeon.

- **Rubio** faced criticism for his "messy" finances. He had a pattern of falling behind on credit card payments, and he mingled personal and political spending, which—although not illegal—enabled Bush and Trump to question his financial judgment.

- Although **Bush** had been considered the leading candidate, a series of missteps bruised him. In the summer, Trump had labelled Bush "low energy," repeating the slur on the campaign trail. The tag stuck.

- When **Trump** entered the race in June, he took a hardline stance on immigration, proclaiming, "When Mexico sends its people, . . . they're sending people [who are] bringing drugs, they're bringing crime. They're rapists." Bush and other candidates were appalled.

- **Fiorina**, former CEO of Hewlett Packard and a Stanford graduate from a privileged background, peddled a story about rising from secretary to CEO that was misleading, at best. Under her direction, Hewlett Packard faltered and she was forced to resign.

Clinton and her experienced team were ill prepared for serious competition from **Sanders**, a septuagenarian and self-described "democratic socialist." **O'Malley**, a youthful 52, was a long shot, but he was not ready to drop out. Photos of a shirtless O'Malley drew eyeballs on the internet, and even serious news sources, such as the *Washington Post* and the *Atlantic*, covered O'Malley's abs.

Gunning for Debate

December 10, 2015

"The Donald" is a demagogue,
A xenophobic camera hog.
"Pack your bags and go away.
Stay outside the U.S.A.!"
That's his anti-terror plan—
A Muslim inbound-travel ban.

The theme of Trump's extreme regime
Brings to mind another scheme—
Internment for the Japanese
To "make us safe" and cure unease.

But help! We face a larger threat,
A bigger group we need to vet:
White Christian men who live alone
Are sadly more than Muslims prone
To kill and maim in random acts.
You don't believe me? Check the facts!

And deadlier than all the others
Are white men living with their mothers!

So round 'em up and ship 'em out.
We'll all be safer, have no doubt!
What, you think that's not allowed?
We've learned from Trump; we won't be cowed!
We'll put them in a *data*base!
We'll make I.D.s that show their face!
For those still living with their moms—
It's not just guns; they're into bombs!
For them a smart computer chip
Will catch them at a faster clip!

Our database will flag a name
And then in pulsing text proclaim,
"This loner guy is very white
He'll take his gun and find a site—
A movie, church, perhaps a school—
Don't let a shotgun be his tool!"

Oh, you interrupted me
You say you strongly disagree?
You say a person's lawful right
To keep and bear a gun's airtight?
You say a no-fly guy can buy
A gun because we can't deny
His right to cherish and adore
A weapon meant for waging war?

The NRA's influenced you
With voodoo through Amendment Two!
Your fetish for that fitful clause
Would give the Founding Fathers pause.
In fact, they'd rise as one and say,
"You're off the mark now, NRA!"

▶ A turning point in the campaign came on December 2, 2015, when a husband and wife murdered 14 people in San Bernardino, California, at a county-government holiday party. The husband was born in the United States to Pakistani-immigrant parents. His wife, from Pakistan and Saudi Arabia, was a legal resident of the U.S. The FBI found that they were inspired by Islamic terrorism and jihadism.

At a campaign rally shortly after the shooting, Trump called for "a total and complete shutdown of Muslims entering the United States until our country's representatives can figure out what the hell is going on." Earlier, Trump had implied that he would require immigrant Muslims to register in a database and obtain a special form of identification.

Some observers, especially on social media, dryly noted that no one had advocated banning white Christian men when one of them went on a shooting rampage, as a disturbed loner had done just a week earlier at a Colorado Planned Parenthood site, or as the Sandy Hook Elementary School shooter, a misfit living with his mother, had done in December 2012.

The day after the San Bernardino slaughter, the Senate rejected, largely along party lines, measures introduced by Democrats to expand background checks and to prevent people on terrorist watch lists, including the no-fly list, from purchasing firearms. The NRA applauded, and Trump continued his tirades in support of gun rights and a Muslim ban, eliciting wild cheers at his rallies.

Year-End State of the Race

December 31, 2015

George Pataki's bowing out,
Bush's future is in doubt,
Cruz is raking in the dough,
Fiorina's going slow,
Carson's major staffers quit,
Donald Trump is still a hit,
Marco's still in fighting range....
Next year, though, this *all* may change!

▶ Although many were appalled by Trump's Muslim-ban proposal, it hit a chord and his popularity climbed. Other candidates lost ground. Former New York Governor George Pataki, a longshot contender, dropped out of the race on December 29; his poll numbers were close to zero and he had never qualified for the primetime debates. In contrast, about 35% of likely Republican voters favored Trump in late December. Cruz, with improved fundraising, was next, at 18%–19%, and Rubio was third, at 11%–14%. Bush and Fiorina were slumping, with poll numbers in the low to middle single digits. Carson averaged 9%, and his campaign was in disarray, with key staff members resigning on New Year's Eve.

Calm Before the Storm

January 1, 2016

Oh, the New Year's begun
And I slept until one.
I watched rom-coms and fluff,
No political stuff!
Yes, I rested instead
For the year that's ahead!

▶ After witnessing the colorful debates and rallies of 2015, some political obsessives needed a holiday respite.

Venom

January 15, 2016

By "birthering" Cruz
Trump finally got boos.
He thinks he can't lose,
But the venom he spews
May cease to amuse
The crowd that he woos.

▶ January 2016 was action-packed, with its buildup to the first two nominating contests—the Iowa caucuses on February 1 and the New Hampshire primary on February 9. With Cruz nearing and sometimes surpassing Trump in December and January Iowa polls, the real estate magnate stepped up his vitriol, questioning whether Cruz, born in Canada to an American mother, was eligible for the presidency. Grassroots conservatives jeered Trump for his "birther" attacks on Cruz.

A Sanders Surge

January 19, 2016

Bernie's too repetitive,
Same ol' stuff in all debates,
But he's now competitive,
Catching up in early states!

▶ The Democratic race was heating up. Sanders's poll numbers were on the upswing, not only in his neighboring state of New Hampshire, where he held a wide lead, but also in Iowa, where he and Clinton were neck and neck. (Clinton had a double-digit lead in Iowa as late as mid-December.) Sanders recited the same points, almost verbatim, in every debate and speech, but his fans didn't seem to mind.

O'Malley Dallies

January 19, 2016

Though he hasn't made a blunder
Many people ask and wonder
Why he lingers in the race
When he's stuck in far last place.
Does he have an ego need
Shouting, "Martin, don't concede"?
Does he want to make his name
With 15 minutes' worth of fame?
Does he have a secret goal
To gain the party's VP role?
Bern and Hill don't really care
Whether Martin's even there.

▶ O'Malley campaigned and participated in the Democratic debate in January, but dropped out of the race on February 1.

An Incoherent Adherent

January 19, 2016

The demagogue ditz
Who gave Democrats fits
Backs the real-estate creep—
Pray she *won't* be his Veep!

▶ 2008 vice-presidential candidate Sarah Palin, a favorite of grass-roots conservatives, tea partiers, and evangelical Christians, endorsed Trump on January 19 in Iowa, perhaps giving him a boost among the evangelicals Cruz was courting. Her endorsement speech, however, was disjointed and confusing, and even Trump seemed perplexed by it.

Boos Cruz

January 20, 2016

Senators abhor him,
Iowans adore him.
No one sane is for him!
Me, I just ignore him!

▶ Cruz was sometimes called the "most hated man" in the Senate (even by Republicans) because of his self-aggrandizement, polarizing stances, and disregard for colleagues. Not a single senator had endorsed him. Nonetheless, he was drawing enthusiastic crowds in Iowa, and his poll numbers climbed. (The challenge in this poem was to create four rhyming lines. The key rhyme is the stressed syllable before the unstressed word "him.")

Yikes, *Is It* Mike's *Turn?*

January 24, 2016

An advocate of gun control
He's very hard to pigeonhole—
He backs a woman's right to choose
And battles Bernie's banking views....
Will Mayor Bloomberg join the fun
And make a presidential run?

► As the campaign reached a fever pitch, Michael Bloomberg, the former New York City mayor, contemplated entering the race. Calm and rational, he wanted to counter what he viewed as the extremes of Trump and Sanders. Ultimately, Bloomberg decided not to run because he thought his candidacy would hurt Clinton's.

Good Job, Winter Storm Jonas!

January 25, 2016

Jonas shut down *all* DC
Better than the GOP!

▶ Threatening to close (or actually closing) the government is a Congressional GOP scorched-earth tactic. Proving that Mother Nature is more potent than politics, winter storm Jonas (also known as Snowzilla) buried much of the mid-Atlantic and Northeast in more than two feet of snow, essentially closing down Washington, DC, including its entire mass transit system.

On-the-Take Mistake?

January 25, 2016

"Wall Street bankers, pay me, please,
Huge six-figure speaking fees!
On the stump I'll say you *stink*."
(Mr. Blankfein, wink, wink.)

▶ In January, Sanders started criticizing Clinton for the lucrative speeches she gave to Wall Street firms. His staff had wanted him to raise the issue in the fall, but he preferred a more policy-oriented campaign. By January, however, he was persuaded. He claimed that Clinton was too close to Wall Street to be trusted to rein in the big banks. Goldman Sachs alone, with Lloyd Blankfein at its helm, had paid Clinton $675,000 for three speeches. Clinton insisted she would still be able to curtail the industry's excesses, but she refused to release the content of her speeches. Even some of her supporters were disappointed that she made well-paid speeches to large banks when she knew she might soon run for president.

Republican Establishment Embarrassment

January 27, 2016

The mainstream GOP is mad
That Trump is not a passing fad,
It's *their* own *fault* they can't curtail him:
They set the stage with Sarah Palin.
Undisciplined, unqualified,
She drew big crowds and often lied,
Attracting, with self-righteous pride,
Our nation's angry underside.

▶ Trump's popularity irritated mainstream Republicans. Some found his anti-immigration rhetoric too inflammatory. Others claimed he was not a true conservative, dedicated to limited government, but instead, a crude, angry populist with authoritarian inclinations and a danger to the party.

If He's Afraid of Megyn, How Will He Handle Merkel or Khamenei?

January 27, 2016

The last debate before the caucus
Perhaps won't be so loud and raucous.
Yes, Trump withdrew 'cause "bloody Kelly"
Might turn the bully into jelly.

▶ After Fox News, the host of the final Republican debate before the Iowa caucuses, announced that journalist Megyn Kelly would be a moderator, Trump refused to participate. At the first debate, back in August, Kelly had asked Trump tough questions, and the next day he claimed that she had treated him unfairly, with "blood coming out of her whatever." Cruz accused Trump of being "afraid of Megyn Kelly." Withdrawing from a debate at such an important time, with the Iowa and New Hampshire contests around the corner, was unprecedented.

Iowa Headline

February 1, 2016

Far-right Texan, foreign birth,
Beats the lout with high net worth!
Expert pollsters can't predict
Whom those pesky voters pick.

Cruz-ing to Victory

February 2, 2016

Now Iowa is done.
Trump's baffled that Cruz won
And Rubio was close,
Yet Trump is not morose.
He *still* predicts he'll win.
But few believe his spin.

▶ Cruz won the Iowa caucuses with almost 28% of the vote, even though the most recent polls had shown Trump with a five-point lead. Trump was second, with 24%, and Rubio was a close third, with 23%. No other candidate reached double digits. Evangelical Christians helped propel Cruz to victory, and his success was a blow to Trump, who had unceasingly crowed that he'd win in Iowa.

Question for Debate

February 4, 2016

Can Bernie's pack of young idealists
Beat Clinton's flock of aging realists?
Though Clinton has the party's backing,
She *can't* send Bernie Sanders packing!

▶ Although Iowa polls showed Clinton comfortably leading Sanders in November and December, by January her position was precarious. Sanders was even *ahead* in some polls. Clinton ended up winning Iowa by only 0.2%—49.8% to 49.6%. In New Hampshire, Sanders's lead began to climb in early January. Clinton, backed by much of the party establishment, led among older voters, whereas Sanders captivated younger voters and the party's left wing. In response to his popularity with progressives, Clinton described herself as a "progressive who gets things done."

Rubio, What What What What Were You Thinking?

February 7, 2016

Chris Christie plotted your demise
But, Marco, did you realize
Your wacky four-time canned reprise
Helped destroy your recent rise....

▶ Rubio entered the Republican debate in New Hampshire with momentum, after his close third-place finish in Iowa. He had been gaining in New Hampshire polls, with the primary just days away. A strong showing would bolster his claim that he was the mainstream candidate the party should unite around. Indeed, many Republicans were counting on Rubio's speaking skills, youthful energy, and seeming self-composure. But at the February 6 debate in New Hampshire, Christie attacked him viciously and Rubio stumbled badly. In essence, Christie claimed that Rubio was an empty suit who robotically recited smooth lines that his handlers had written for him. Inexplicably, Rubio seemed to prove Christie right. Rubio bizarrely recited a memorized statement, almost word for word, four times during the debate, and the crowd booed. Christie also attacked Rubio for his no-shows at important Senate votes. The New Hampshire debate was the beginning of the end for Rubio, but it also hurt Christie, who came off as caustic and brutish and perhaps insufficiently presidential. (Bullying never seemed to hurt Trump, though.)

Babes for Bernie

February 8, 2016

"Hey, these rallies are better than Tinder or Match.
So hello, Bernie boys, I'm a fabulous catch.
Yes, we're *all* Bernin' up 'cause you guys are so hot!
It's upsetting that Steinem is onto our plot."

▶ In a poll of New Hampshire Democrats about a week before the state's primary, 64% of women under 45 favored Sanders. His popularity with young women disheartened feminist icon Gloria Steinem, 81. In early February, she suggested that young women were backing Sanders so they could meet young men: "When you're young, you're thinking, where are the boys? The boys are with Bernie." Not surprisingly, young women found the comment demeaning. Steinem's apology did little to help; the damage was done and social media erupted in criticism, wonder, and sarcasm.

New Hampshire's Super Primary

February 10, 2016

New Hampshire's done.
It sure was fun
For folks like me
Who'd rather be
Observing brand new voter polls
Than half-time shows at Super Bowls!

▶ Political junkies had eagerly awaited February 9, the day of the New Hampshire primary. That evening, they watched TV pundits scrutinize the results, perhaps unaware that many more Americans had tuned into the Super Bowl two days earlier. The Denver Broncos won, as did Trump and Sanders.

New Hampshire Republican Primary Aftermath

February 10, 2016

Christie's out
Loudmouth lout.
Carly too
Hewlett shrew.
Marco's down
Robot clown.
Bush is stuck
Out of luck.
Donald won
By a ton.
Kasich's rise
Small surprise.
Carson's staying
Always praying.
Cruz awaits
Other states.

▶ The results of the New Hampshire primary changed the Republican race. Trump, the victor, drew 35% of the vote. Christie and Fiorina dropped out after poor showings. Kasich, in second place with almost 16%, performed better than expected, probably because he was the "only adult in the room" in several debates, appealing to the more moderate New England Republicans. Rubio fared far less well than he did in Iowa, at only 10.5%; his robotic performance in the New Hampshire debate a few days earlier clearly damaged him. Although Christie pummeled Rubio in that debate, the New Jersey governor took himself down even further (to 7%), with his pugilistic, off-putting demeanor. Cruz also performed less well than in Iowa, coming in third at about 12%, but he was happy to wait for the upcoming primaries in states with bigger evangelical Christian populations. Carson fared poorly, at only 2%, but decided to stay in the game. On the Democratic side, Sanders won with more than 60% of the vote. Young voters, men, and Independents preferred the Vermont Senator by wide margins, but he did have a neighboring-state advantage. This poem was created as a challenge: be far less verbose than the political commentators, with only three syllables per line.

Brash Clash

February 25, 2016

Last night's GOP debate
Made pro wrestling seem sedate!
The losers in the latest clash
Were passive pundits Wolf and Bash.

▶ The Republican candidates' discourse, never known for a high level of substance, sank to new lows in the February debates. A cnn.com reporter called the February 13 debate the "most bitter and vicious brawl of the 2016 cycle." The *New York Times* described the next debate, the final showdown before the Super Tuesday primaries on March 1, as "the messiest and most confrontational debate of the Republican presidential primary, . . . repeatedly descending into free-for-alls." Cruz and Trump sparred in an almost incoherent shouting match. Rubio attacked Trump for hiring foreign workers and for operating the sham Trump University, and Trump assailed Rubio for his financial problems. Co-moderators Wolf Blitzer and Dana Bash of CNN were unable to contain the commotion. Carson, frustrated by his lack of speaking time, uttered the best line of the debate: "Can somebody attack me, please?"

Magical Intent

February 26, 2016

I don't get "original intent."
How come what the Founding Fathers meant
Always matches ultra far-right views?
Could it be a clever legal ruse?

▶ Praise for U.S. Supreme Court Justice Antonin Scalia, who died on February 13, fostered a rare instance of agreement among the Republican candidates. Rubio, for example, lauded Scalia's life-long efforts to defend the "original meaning of the Constitution," and promised a nominee who looks to "original intent" to resolve constitutional issues. (Scalia's doctrine was actually "originalism," or "original meaning" theory, i.e., what reasonable people living at the time would have understood the meaning of the text to be. "Original intent" holds that the interpretation of the text should be consistent with what the drafters meant at the time.)

A Coarse Endorser

February 28, 2016

The well-known bigot David Duke
Came out for Trump; it's not a fluke,
'Cause Trump incites the basest fears
For cheap applause and mindless cheers.

▶ David Duke, the white supremacist and former Klu Klux Klan grand wizard, announced his support for Trump on February 24. He urged "European-Americans" to
back Trump, maintaining that voting against him would be "treason to your heri-
tage." Duke touted Trump's "strengths" on immigration and on breaking up "Jewish
dominated lobbies and super PACS that are corrupting and controlling American
politics."

Toady Roadie

March 2, 2016

Chris Christie, crude and plump,
Backed fellow bully Donald Trump
For payoff down the road somehow....
The pit bull is a lapdog now!

▶ Christie withdrew from the race on February 10. Although he had been very critical
of Trump, Christie threw his support to him. The New Jersey governor soon became
a sycophant, traipsing after Trump on the campaign trail. At one of Trump's celebra-
tory press conferences, Christie stood behind him during the entire victory speech,
with a dazed, forlorn expression that set Twitter afire with lampoons.

The Once and Future Contender

March 4, 2016

This morning we heard from ex-candidate Mitt,
Who said, for the White House, that Trump isn't fit.
A brokered convention is what we might see
With Romney recycled, the "new" nominee!

▶ After Trump won seven of the eleven Super Tuesday primaries on March 1, efforts by mainstream Republicans to impede him faced a new urgency. Two days after Super Tuesday, 2012 presidential candidate Mitt Romney delivered a scathing critique of Trump, calling him "a phony, a fraud," who has "neither the temperament nor the judgment to be president." As the anti-Trump movement picked up steam, the internet teemed with rumors of an open convention, with a more traditional Republican as the candidate.

Hostility to Civility

March 5, 2016

Marco and Donald, with eyes on the prize,
Fought over sweating and penile size.
Cruz, though combative, avoided that mess.
Kasich's a grownup and thus gets no press.

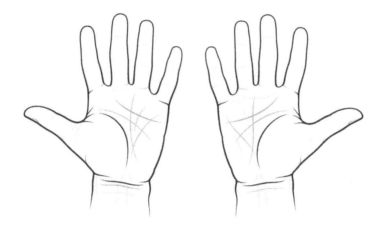

▶ The Republican campaign seemed to become cruder every week. At one rally in late February, Trump made fun of Rubio for heavy sweating. Rubio, in turn, taunted Trump for having "small hands." At the March 3 debate, Trump held out his arms and exclaimed: "Look at those hands. Are those small?" Noting that Rubio had used hand size as a metaphor for another body part, Trump dismissed the contention: "I guarantee you there is no problem." Cruz steered clear of crudeness, but he and Rubio ganged up to attack Trump on his immigration views, business record, and temperament. Trump swatted them away with condescending nicknames: "Little Marco" and "Lyin' Ted." Kasich stayed above the fray and tried futilely to raise the level of discussion.

Much-Anticipated Finale

March 7, 2016

So how could there be yet another debate?
What more could be said to determine their fate?
Yet Sanders and Clinton, they clashed head to head,
While America watched Downton Abbey instead.

▶ By March 6, the day of the Democratic debate in Flint, Michigan, Clinton and Sanders had faced off several times, and many viewers were growing weary of their interactions. Nonetheless, the candidates delivered one of their most confrontational exchanges yet, talking over each other and clashing on the auto industry bailout, trade policy, gun safety, Wall Street ties, and other topics. But sometimes during campaign season, politics takes a back seat. The "Downton Abbey" series finale on PBS drew 9.6 million viewers on March 6. The Democratic debate, hosted on CNN during the "Downton Abbey" finale, drew 5.5 million viewers, the second lowest result for any debate thus far.

History Herstory

March 7, 2016

More than just a White House resident,
In effect, a female president—
She counseled, guided, soldiered on;
Now dauntless Nancy Reagan's gone.

▶ In her 2008 presidential bid, Clinton steered clear of playing up her gender, but this time around, she often mentioned the historic opportunity to become the first female president of United States. On March 6, the same day as the Clinton–Sanders debate in Michigan, the death of another powerful First Lady made the news.

Misreading Michigan

March 10, 2016

The polls showed Clinton widely leading
But Sanders ended up succeeding.
Yes, Bernie wound up very strong,
And every expert got it wrong.

▶ Polls conducted shortly before the Michigan Democratic primary on March 8 showed Clinton winning by an average of 21.4 points. Even so, Sanders won, beating Clinton by 1.5 points. It was one of the biggest polling mistakes in the history of presidential primaries.

Liar, Liar, Pantsuits on Fire!

March 11, 2016

Yes, Hillary's tactics in two thousand eight
Made many Obama supporters irate.
She's at it again now, distorting the truth,
And angering Bernie's alliance of youth.
She'll need them to vote if she runs in the fall,
She'd better re-tune or she might lose it all.

▶ With Sanders more popular than expected, Clinton ramped up her attacks on him, but sometimes she played fast and loose with the facts. For example, she twisted details to imply that Sanders voted against his base's views on immigration and the auto bailout.

Demagogue Hog

March 13, 2016

Anger's brewing
Hatred's stewing
Trump is spewing
Speech that's vile,
Full of bile,
Meant to rile
Chanting hordes
Moving towards
Fascist dreams
Racist themes
Brutal screams.
Donald craves
Frenzied raves
Frantic rants
Fawning chants.
Stop him now
Who knows how?

▶ Unruliness at some of Trump's rallies led to physical clashes, and the violence was increasing. Many observers, including Cruz and Rubio, claimed that Trump's inflammatory rhetoric contributed to the uptick in violence. For example, at a late February rally, Trump bellowed, "I'd like to punch him in the face," referring to a protester. A few months earlier, after Trump fans had kicked and punched an activist who was shouting, "Black lives matter," Trump noted, "Maybe he should have been roughed up, because it was absolutely disgusting what he was doing." Trump also vowed to pay the legal fees of supporters who "knock the crap" out of protesters. At this point, with his multiple primary victories and his lead in the Florida and Illinois polls, Trump was the clear frontrunner, with the Republican establishment helpless to curtail him.

Chicago No-Go

March 14, 2016

The fury Trump induced
In crowds that he seduced
Came crashing home to roost
When a rally that descended
Into fighting was suspended.
Yet Donald, ever brash,
So arrogant and rash,
Deflected all the blame
While keeping rage aflame.

▶ With thousands waiting in a packed arena, Trump's campaign abruptly cancelled a Chicago rally over safety concerns, as protestors and Trump fans erupted in heated clashes. CNN's Jake Tapper asked Trump, as "a fellow American," to "consider dialing down the temperature" at his rallies. Trump refused to take responsibility for the turmoil and violence at his events, ignoring criticism from Republicans who worried that he was inciting animosity that would veer out of control.

March Madness

March 16, 2016

Yes, March sure is madness,
For Marco, it's sadness,
For Kasich, a boost:
His home state produced
A win at long last,
But Donald amassed
So many more votes
And once again gloats.
But Ted is still cruising,
Not thinking of losing.
Just three guys remain
In this shocking campaign.
Will Rubio choose
John Kasich or Cruz?
Unlikely he'll stump
For archrival Trump.
Who next will be gone?
The show will go on.....

▶ After the March 15 Republican primaries, Rubio ended his once-promising campaign. In his home state of Florida, he suffered a devastating loss to Trump. Kasich won in *his* home state, Ohio, but otherwise Trump was the victor, winning North Carolina and Illinois in addition to Florida. Trump and Cruz were neck and neck in Missouri, with Trump ultimately winning by a hair (40.8% to 40.6%).

Merrick Merit

March 16, 2016

Obama chose with care.
Will the GOP still dare
Impede his careful pick?
Their response was pretty quick:
Mitch McConnell said "No *way*
Will Obama have his say.
Let's await the vote this fall,
Let's get ready for a brawl!"

▶ The day after the March 15 primaries, Obama nominated Judge Merrick Garland for the U.S. Supreme Court seat vacated by the death of Antonin Scalia. Less than a week earlier, Republican Senator Orrin Hatch (R-UT) had said that President Obama "could easily name [the moderate] Merrick Garland, who is a fine man," but surmised that the president instead would nominate a candidate who appealed to the liberal Democratic base. Yet when Obama selected Garland, Senate Majority Leader Mitch McConnell (R-KY) and his fellow Republicans, in an unprecedented move, refused to consider Garland's nomination, not even holding a hearing. They declared that the next president should fill the vacancy, even though Obama still had ten months left in office.

Fall Gall

March 17, 2016

If it's Donald versus Clinton, I will hibernate this fall.
The campaigns will be so vicious I may want to flee it all.
I'll go trekking in the mountains where the internet can't reach
Or I'll pack a dozen novels and I'll settle on a beach,
But perhaps I'm now an addict who will need her newsy fix....
Are there pills that can prepare me for a blitz of dirty tricks?

▶ In mid-March, well before the nominations were finalized, the Trump campaign aired a nasty ad against Clinton. If she became the Democratic nominee, would she respond in kind? Few looked forward to a malicious general-election season, and many wondered how low they'd go.

Memo to Politicians

March 22, 2016

My heart goes out to Brussels on this senseless, tragic day.
I hope you don't exploit this in your zealous, selfish way.
Don't agitate or rant or try to bait your chanting herds.
Be careful with your conduct; aim for wisdom with your words.

▶ On March 22, 2016, terrorists set off bombs in Brussels, Belgium—two at the airport and one at a subway station. Thirty-two people were killed, with more than 300 injured. The bombings, the deadliest act of terrorism in Belgium's history, stunned Brussels, the headquarters of the European Union and NATO. The frontrunners did not heed the advice in this poem (not that they read it). Trump tweeted, "Incompetent Hillary, despite the horrible attack in Brussels today, wants borders to be weak and open—and let the Muslims flow in." Hillary responded, "The last thing we need, my friends, are leaders who incite more fear."

National Enquiring Minds Want to Know

March 25, 2016

So who would want to sleep with Ted?
I'd rather walk on nails instead.
And who believes this tabloid tale?
For some it seems beyond the pale.
Yes, tabloids sometimes love to tell
Salacious news they know will sell,
But from the Edwards mess we learned
That though they may seem unconcerned
With truth and facts they sometimes tell
The sorry truth and tell it well.
The *New York Times* then has to cite
The tabloid rag that got it right!

▶ In late March, the *National Enquirer*'s front page blared, "Cruz's 5 Secret Mistresses!" A red banner at the top proclaimed, "It's over for pervy Ted." Although the *Enquirer* is known for publishing tawdry, dubious stories that mainstream newspapers won't touch, sometimes it is proven right. For example, the *Enquirer* was the first paper to report on 2004 Democratic VP candidate John Edwards's affair and "love child." Later, mainstream news sources, including the *New York Times*, did give credit to the *Enquirer* for breaking the story. Because Trump is friends with the CEO of the *Enquirer*'s parent company, some speculated that Trump's team was behind the Cruz story.

Democracy is Messy

March 26, 2016

Democracy is messy, as our politicians know,
But this year's GOP campaign has hit a brand new low.
Some are hoping for a brokered nomination come July
But the angry base of voters, they would never let that fly.
And Donald said to Fox he won't engage in more debates
So now we need another way to settle on their fates....
Why not send them to an island where there isn't much to eat
And take away their cellphones so that none of them can tweet!
No reporters will be lurking, asking questions out of spite,
Instead there'll be mosquitoes that will linger, sting or bite.
They'll be far away from Flint although with water far less clean,
No Pepsi, Koch or PAC and no political machine.
To keep out thugs and riffraff they'll build walls of trees and skins
And whoever comes out strongest is the candidate who wins!

▶ Trump and Cruz continued to attack each other, reducing the Republican campaign to the level of schoolyard taunts or *Survivor*-style reality TV. In mid-March, frontrunner Trump told Fox News that he wouldn't participate in the debate that was scheduled for the following week. Kasich wouldn't join the debate unless Trump did, so Fox News canceled it. Meanwhile, speculation about a brokered or contested Republican convention continued. Trump was still unpopular with traditional small-government conservatives, including Charles and David Koch (pronounced "Coke"), the billionaire brothers known for funding libertarian and right-leaning causes.

Spouse Wars

March 30, 2016

Mrs. Trump was a model, perfectly dressed.
Mrs. Cruz is a banker, sometimes depressed.
If one's fitness for the White House
Rests on having wed the right spouse,
Here's a nagging question, thus far unaddressed:
How does BILL perform on such a vital test?!

▶ Shortly before the Utah Republican caucuses, an anti-Trump super-PAC posted an ad on social media that featured a seemingly nude photo of Trump's wife, Melania, from a modeling shoot more than 15 years earlier. The ad admonished: "Meet Melania Trump, your next First Lady. Or, you could support Ted Cruz on Tuesday." Cruz disavowed any connection to the ad and the PAC. Trump nonetheless retaliated, first by threatening to "spill the beans" on Ted's wife, Heidi Cruz. (This was the same day as the terrorist attack in Brussels.) She had already spoken publicly about her experience with depression, and some thought Trump was threatening to attack or embarrass her for that. Next, Trump tweeted side-by-side photos of the two would-be First Ladies: Melania in a photo-edited glamour shot, and Heidi in an unflattering candid photo. Cruz criticized Trump for his low-level attack on Heidi and won the Utah caucuses by a wide margin. Kasich came in second and Trump third, slowing the frontrunner's momentum.

Scarlet Letters

April 3, 2016

Back when he was Donald Juan
Frolicking from dusk to dawn
With beauty queens and models too
I'd wager there were quite a few
Who exercised their right to choose
And Donald then had pro-choice views.
He now adopts a right-wing voice
Insisting that he's anti-choice.
He even mused that women who
Obtain abortions should go through
A punishment—but who knows what?
Communal branding as a slut?
Or scarlet A's on every dress
And shotgun-threats to reassess?
The groups that find abortion wrong
Agreed his words were much too strong,
So Trump recanted pretty quickly,
But still this issue's very prickly.

▶ In a town-hall discussion on MSNBC, Trump said that if abortion becomes illegal, women who have the procedure should face "some form of punishment." After much criticism (including from anti-choice groups), Trump backtracked, saying that "the doctor ... performing this illegal act upon a woman would be held legally responsible, not the woman." He said he is anti-abortion, and the issue should be left to the states. Yet in the late 1980s, Trump co-sponsored a dinner honoring a former president of NARAL Pro-Choice America. In a 1999 interview, Trump maintained that he was "very pro-choice," but by 2011, his public position had changed.

Play Ball, CNN!

April 12, 2016

Yay, baseball's back and I'm so glad!
This voting season drives me mad
And baseball makes a fine distraction
Without a right- or left-wing faction.
Republicans and Democrats
Wear matching tees and baseball hats.
Together they applaud and scream,
Encouraging the local team.
Debates are over strikes and balls,
Not taxes, guns, or building walls.
Perhaps the ump behind home plate
Could moderate our next debate!

▶ With the start of baseball season, fans were able to enjoy frequent breaks from politics.

Bad Call

April 13, 2016

The famous ERA opponent
Is now a Donald Trump proponent.
Miss Schlafly (still alive, it seems)
Believes our country's baseball teams
Should ban Hispanics, Japanese,
And anyone from overseas.
The "golden age" that's in her dreams
Is from the age of all-white teams.
Alas, there was a lousy ump
When Phyllis Schlafly stumped for Trump.

▶ On March 11, Phyllis Schlafly, the conservative activist and vocal Equal Rights Amendment (ERA) opponent, endorsed Trump at a rally in St. Louis. Her endorsement brought attention to a recent radio talk in which she yearned for baseball's "good old days," when players were "American-born" and "[rose] through the ranks of Little League." She suggested banning foreign-born players from Major League Baseball, and fondly recalled attending a World Series game between the St. Louis Cardinals and St. Louis Browns in 1944, three years before Jackie Robinson broke the color barrier. (Schlafly did not live to see Trump's victory; she died at 92 on September 5, 2016.)

Ecstatic/Pragmatic

April 18, 2016

Oh, you "Bernie or Bust" folks might have to get real.
Yes, your guy is a gutsy, progressive ideal—
He discusses the issues, not Hillary's emails,
Or Benghazi or Bill's little problems with females.
But on numerous issues important today,
You are closer to Clinton than what you might say.
For example, you're likely to show your support
For the same type of jurists to serve on the Court,
And you favor affordable care for one's health
Irrespective of prior conditions or wealth,
And reducing the NRA's powerful hold
On the cowards who vote to keep guns uncontrolled,
And a workable plan to address immigration,
Not a Mexican wall and incessant damnation,
So if Clinton's the winner of delegate math,
Please do *not* run away in a self-righteous wrath.
You do *not* need to rally or cheer her out loud,
But you're closer to her than the GOP crowd.
So although there is value in being ecstatic,
In November consider a switch to pragmatic,
And acknowledge she's better than Donald or Cruz.
Hold your pride, hold your nose, but do *not* let her lose.

▶ With her strong victory in the New York primary, Clinton grew closer to clinching the Democratic nomination. "I believe there is much more that unites us than divides us," she said in her victory speech, in a gesture to Sanders supporters. If she were to win the nomination, what would Sanders voters do? Some, claiming she was too conservative or too "Republican," vowed to stay home on Election Day. Others thought the "Bernie or Bust" devotees should reassess their stubborn stance.

April 26 Primary Results

April 27, 2016

The Northeast coast
Said Ted was toast,
And Donald swept
While Kasich wept.
Ted needed press
For new success
And so he named
A female famed
For spewing hate
To be his mate.
Though Clinton bragged
And Bernie lagged,
He vowed to stay
With hopes to sway
The platform's aims
And keep the flames
A-Berning bright.
Might he unite
The Bernie bros
With Clinton's pros?
It seems, in sum,
That she'll become
The nominee
And then we'll see
A nasty brawl
With Trump come fall!

▶ Trump swept the five April 26 primaries—Pennsylvania, Maryland, Rhode Island, Connecticut, and Delaware—with landslides of more than 30 percentage points above his remaining rivals, Cruz and Kasich. Cruz fared particularly poorly in the Northeast, where his extreme conservatism and emphasis on faith did not play well. To generate publicity, he named Carly Fiorina as his running mate. Kasich was unable to beat Trump even in Connecticut, where Republicans tend to be moderate. On the Democratic side, Sanders won only in Rhode Island and fell further behind Clinton, who bested him in Connecticut, Maryland, Pennsylvania, and Delaware. The big wins for Trump and Clinton on April 26 intensified their auras of inevitability, and they attacked each in their primary-night speeches, as if practicing for autumn.

Trump Thumps Chumps!

May 4, 2016

Yes, Cruz dropped out and Kasich too—
For Donald Trump, that's quite a coup.
His rage came first, with flying sparks,
Then nasty nicknames hit their marks.
"Little Marco," sluggish Jeb—
His mocking tone would never ebb.
He called Ted "Lyin'" till the end
And claimed Ted's dad was Oswald's friend!
Pretending Kasich wasn't there
Just heightened John's polite despair.
Trump's spite and might, they worked liked charms,
And that should set off loud alarms
For Clinton's smug yet scared campaign,
Where staffers, if they've half a brain,
Had better have some tactics planned
To counter Donald's toxic brand.

▶ On May 4, Trump won the Indiana primary by a decisive margin—53% to Cruz's 37% and Kasich's 8%. Cruz and Kasich withdrew from the race, and Trump—the brash, improbable candidate—became the presumptive nominee.

Billions in Free Publicity!

May 17, 2016

I turned on CNN
And there he was again
I switched to PBS
And saw more ceaseless press.
On MSNBC
Who'd you think I'd see?
Yes, even lefty Maddow
Cannot escape his shadow.
The front page of the *Times*
Has chronicled his climbs.
Its op-ed pages bray,
Quite often twice a day:
The golden-haired tycoon
Is just a vain buffoon
Obsessed with women's looks.
He angers David Brooks.
His GOP foe Mitt
Insists that he's a twit.
He gets to free-rein schmooze
On Sunday morning's news.
A hothead heavy hitter,
He posts harangues on Twitter;
They frequently are sordid
But always get reported.
Perhaps he lacks finesse,
But he's a master of the press!

▶ On many evenings, TV-news viewers could change channels repeatedly in a futile search for a respite from Trump coverage. As early as mid-March, a media-tracking firm reported that he had received close to $2 billion in free publicity (broadcast, print, and online), far more than any other candidate, while spending less on television advertising—usually a campaign's biggest expense—than the others had. By Election Day, studies showed that Trump had received more than $5 billion in free publicity.

News Roundup Before the California and New Jersey Primaries

June 7, 2016

A judge from Indiana who's of Mexican descent
Can surely try a case without an anti-Donald bent,
Yet Trump is digging in his heels and sticking by his word,
While Marco, Ted, and Newt agree he's hateful and absurd.
And AP in advance proclaimed that Clinton clinched the race,
But Bernie kept on keepin' on to make his rebel case.
The Dems might be too fractured in the fall to win the prize;
The victors now are networks with their ratings on the rise.

▶ In early June, Donald Trump claimed that an American-born U.S. District Court judge, Gonzalo Curiel, would be unable to preside fairly over a fraud lawsuit against Trump University because of his Mexican ancestry. In the face of sharp criticism (including from prominent Republicans), Trump didn't back down; he repeatedly defended his charge. Meanwhile, on the Democratic front, political watchers expected Clinton to clinch the nomination after the June 7 primaries in New Jersey, California, and four other states. She needed just 23 more delegates. The Sanders camp asked the media *not* to make any announcements until after the polls closed in California. But on Monday evening, a day *before* the primaries, the Associated Press (AP) unexpectedly called the Democratic race for Clinton, in part because the news agency had surveyed superdelegates and found enough who backed her. Sanders supporters and others maintained that "pre-announcing" the winner suppressed votes and hurt his chances in the next day's primaries, noting that superdelegates were allowed to change their minds up to and even during the Democratic Convention in July.

Irony

June 8, 2016

Though Donald's speeches are cartoonish, void of any heft,
He struck with shocking substance, hitting Clinton from the *left*.
She's too hawkish, Donald shouted, emulating Sanders.
She favored job-death NAFTA, but she changes tunes and panders.
Like Bernie, Trump declared the superdelegates unfair.
Yes, Trump may capture Bernie voters—Hillary, BEWARE!

▶ Trump and Sanders offered very different political views, but on some issues, they were aligned to Clinton's left.

The Blood-Spangled Banner

June 14, 2016 (Flag Day)

These tragic acts of wrath and hate
Are likely to proliferate
When men can saunter through a store
And buy a gun conceived for war,
When lies the NRA has spread
Speak louder than the Newtown dead,
When fear of NRA disdain
Numbs Congress to Orlando's pain.
Assault guns, banned in '94,
Are not illegal anymore.
The "right to bear" was misconstrued;
The prudent ban was not renewed.
A gun not meant for sport or play,
A gun designed for human prey,
A gun envisioned to destroy,
Is sold as if it were a toy.
The GOP should be ashamed
That gun-rights zealots have them tamed.
A silent moment's not enough
When laws are needed, sane and tough.

▶ On June 12, a gunman killed 49 people and wounded 53 in an attack inside an Orlando, Florida, nightclub that catered to a mostly gay and Hispanic crowd. He was armed with a semi-automatic rifle and a semi-automatic pistol. Although he claimed allegiance to ISIS during the shooting, investigations showed that he was a home-grown extremist with no direct connection to the group. The next day, Speaker Paul Ryan (R-WI) led the House in a moment of silence to honor the victims, but the Republicans still refused to stand up to the NRA and take action on gun safety. House Minority Leader Nancy Pelosi (D-CA) spoke for many when she said that Democrats have had "enough of having one minute ... of silence on the floor, and then ... no [legislative] action" after repeated mass shootings.

Brexit

June 29, 2016

Oh, will they stay or will they go?
The British people let us know!
But will they suffer from remorse?
The common wisdom is "of course."
Confused derision transfixed France
While Putin did a joyful dance
And Greece was gripped by fear and doubt
While Brussels snorted "Just get out."
The Scottish, vowing to remain,
Viewed Donald's golf course with disdain
So will there be another vote?
Can Merkel keep it all afloat,
This dream of Europe as a whole,
Connected through a common goal?
Perhaps that vision now is dying,
But E.U.'s aims are still worth trying.
The British have a gift for drama,
But better Shakespeare than this trauma.

▶ On June 23, the United Kingdom surprised the world—especially Europe—by voting to leave the European Union (E.U.). The vote in favor of "Brexit" (a coinage merging "Britain" and "exit") was 52% to 48%. At the time, one astute political observer (my mother) said, "If the U.K. can vote to leave the European Union, then Trump can win the U.S. presidency." Countries reacted differently to Brexit, as this poem reports. Unsurprisingly, Clinton opposed Brexit and Trump favored it.

Email Travails

July 7, 2016

I was sick of her emails
And the unending details,
Like the private home server,
And the GOP's fervor
To attack and unnerve her
While she fought to preserve her
Clear-cut claim on the traits
Shared by top heads of states.

Have her knowledge and trust
Been transformed into dust
By the FBI's claim
That she must take the blame
For her blithe immaturity
In regarding security
With the level of care
That she gives to her hair?

P.S. Clinton fans, chill,
I will vote for her still.

▶ Clinton's use of a private email server while Secretary of State was, as we all know, the subject of an FBI investigation and a heated topic on the campaign trail. Trump often led raucous choruses of "lock her up" at his rallies. Sanders famously said, "I'm sick of hearing about her damn emails," preferring to discuss substantive policy issues. On July 5, FBI Director James Comey announced that he would *not* recommend criminal charges against Clinton because there was no evidence that she had intentionally transmitted or mishandled classified information. Even so, he was very critical of her, maintaining that she was "extremely careless" in her handling of sensitive, highly classified materials. With the Democratic National Convention just a few weeks away, Republicans jumped on Comey's assessment, claiming that it showed Clinton lacked the judgment to be president.

Anguish in Black and Blue

July 10, 2016

A minor traffic stop and death.
A Baton Rouge man's sad last breath.
A sniper filled with hate and malice
Assassinates police in Dallas.
For blue and black lives lost, we grieve;
For lives cut short for naught, we seethe.
Our twisted history of race
And easy weapons marketplace
Ignited in a brutal week;
That's not the country that we seek.
These bloody acts, no aberration,
Should not define our anxious nation.

▶ In July, in the course of just two days, two fatal police shootings of black men kindled public outrage. Both were captured on video and shared on social media. The first victim was shot in front of a convenience store in Baton Rouge, Louisiana, on July 5, and the second was killed during a traffic stop near St. Paul, Minnesota, on July 6. On July 7, at the end of a peaceful demonstration in Dallas, Texas, to protest the shootings, a gunman killed five police officers. Police then killed the shooter with a robot-delivered bomb.

Later in July, the parties held their nominating conventions.

PART TWO

The General Election Campaign

Three-and-One-Half Months to Go

On July 19, 2016, at the Republican National Convention in Cleveland, Trump became the Republican nominee for president. Plans for protest votes and walkouts never materialized, but not every major speaker endorsed him.

On July 26, 2016, at the Democratic National Convention in Philadelphia, Clinton became the first woman to receive the presidential nomination from a major political party. Some Sanders backers protested and refused to get behind Clinton, even though Sanders himself had thrown his support to her.

Trump had a post-convention bounce in the polls, but Clinton's was bigger, and she was widely viewed as the likely winner in November.

DISPATCHES FROM THE REPUBLICAN NATIONAL CONVENTION

The Art of the Steal
July 19, 2016

A stunning white designer dress,
A lovely speech, no sign of stress,
Some platitudes, but I digress,
In general, a poised address,
Designed to placate and impress,
And deemed at first a great success.
But soon ... an unpredicted mess
That Trump's campaign could not finesse,
With Donald's damsel in distress!
Yes, Twitter beat the mainstream press
In finding words that more or less
Were copied from a fine address
Michelle delivered with noblesse.
They hate Obama; nonetheless,
They cribbed from him to gain success.

▶ On the first day of the Republican National Convention, Trump's wife, Melania, spoke from the podium in front of 23 million TV viewers. She rarely addressed the public, and Trump wanted her to be flawless. At first, her speech seemed successful, but soon there was an uproar: it turned out that several stirring passages from Melania's speech were near-replicas of Michelle Obama's words at the 2012 Democratic National Convention.

Cruz-ing, Not Losing

July 21, 2016

You've got to admire the courage of Cruz—
He spoke to a chorus of resolute boos.
Chris Christie may suffer from brownnoser blues,
But Ted is no toady; he sticks to his views.
In fact, that's his downfall; we heard him debate,
And he was unswerving in spouting his hate,
And callous positions on immigrants' fate,
And scorn for the splitting of church and of state.
But Cruz is undaunted by public rebuke;
His RNC discourse was hardly a fluke.
He still has supporters; in fact, he has plenty,
And this was just stagecraft for two thousand twenty.

▶ Although Cruz gave a speech at the Republican National Convention (RNC), he did
not endorse Trump.

DISPATCHES FROM THE DEMOCRATIC NATIONAL CONVENTION

No Unity With Impunity
July 25, 2016

Debbie Wasserman Schultz—she was booed off the stage
In an early display of the Sanders camp's rage.
Oh, the Dems need to show they're a party united,
And that Bernie's endorsement is not unrequited.

▶ On July 22, just days before the Democratic National Convention, WikiLeaks released emails from the Democratic National Committee (DNC) that revealed efforts by chair Debbie Wasserman Schultz (D-FL) and others to undermine Sanders's campaign. The leaked emails ruined the Democrats' wish to display party unity at their convention. (Sanders had bowed out and endorsed Clinton two weeks earlier, and he was able to include some of his planks in the party's platform.) Wasserman Schultz resigned as chair of the DNC before the convention began. She still gave a speech to the delegates from her home state of Florida, but the audience jeered. Democrats alleged that Russia was behind the leaked emails as part of an effort to derail Clinton. Later, the U.S. intelligence community expressed "high confidence" that Russia had indeed hacked the emails and supplied them to WikiLeaks.

Convention News Highlights

July 26, 2016

Corey Booker delivered a soaring oration,
A tryout for upcoming roles in our nation,
And for once Sarah Silverman wasn't obscene—
On the DNC stage she made sure to keep clean.
Al Franken returned to his comedy roots,
Dismayed with the Senate's unending disputes.
Some hackers from Russia leaked DNC emails
With pro-Clinton bias in numerous details,
Confirming what Bernie's camp always suspected.
The risk was they'd grow even more disaffected,
But their man took the stage to sing Hillary's praises
And he said she's now with him on minimum raises
And healthcare and trade and on college tuition,
So Bernie achieved a good chunk of his mission.
But the hit of the night, when the whole hall took notice,
Was the powerful speech from the elegant FLOTUS.
Our leaders, she said, should be models for kids,
And our country is great; it is *not* on the skids.
A divisive dystopia clearly is wrong
And a country united is one that is strong.

▶ The convention's inaugural day featured a parade of speakers, from comedians to politicians to, in Senator Al Franken's (D-MN) case, politicians who were once comedians. First Lady Michelle Obama's speech—a refutation of Trump's hateful, divisive rhetoric—was especially memorable.

The Thrill of Bill

July 27, 2016

Grand speech-master Bill gave a talk for his wife,
A hagiographic account of her life.
From ill first responders to children in need,
She champions others, in word and in deed.
Devouring popcorn and wine on my couch,
I clung to his words but I felt like a slouch.
In the time that it took me to press the remote
Noble Hillary registered thousands to vote.
As a student I dreamt of a beachfront vacation
But Miss Rodham flew south to confront segregation.
They "met cute" in classes they took while at Yale.
He wooed her, she spurned him, his first epic fail,
But the third time he asked for her hand, she said yes,
And they started their lifetime of triumph and stress.
So if he's installed as our nation's "First Lad,"
Will we fret if his taste in fine china is bad?
Or perhaps he will help her with China and trade
And the TPP pledge she may rue having made.
Bill is older and wiser now—will he behave?
Just think of the love and attention he'll crave.
Will America see the good Bill or the bad,
A "First Gentleman" ally or rowdy "First Cad"?

▶ Bill Clinton's speech at the Democratic National Convention was one long valentine
to his wife, the "best darn change maker." He recounted her decades of public service and her tireless efforts to make life better for children, women, minorities, the
poor, the disabled, 9/11 first responders, and others. Even as a student, she helped
others: during summer vacations, she interviewed migrant workers, uncovered il-
legally segregated schools in Alabama, and registered Mexican-American voters in
Texas. He seemed to nominate her for secular sainthood, making it easy for the rapt
audience to forget her shortcomings and challenges, such as her about-face on the
Trans-Pacific Partnership (TPP) and her "troubles" with Bill.

Hillary's Night

July 29, 2016

She is not a great speaker like Bill or Obama.
She is often encumbered by flare-ups and drama.
In a rare note of candor, she made a disclaimer,
And admitted she isn't a gifted campaigner.
Once in office she toils and makes contributions,
And she crosses the aisle to craft joint solutions.
Her Republican colleagues have praised her in private,
And their malice subsides; when she runs they revive it.
One wonders how Clinton has learned to survive it.
Her endless resilience, you've got to high-five it.
The convention's last night was her grand coronation,
Er, I mean she accepted the Dem's nomination.
On her forty-year journey's sublime culmination,
Would Hillary furnish a fitting oration?
The presenters before her all carried her water,
They were cogent and strong, and at last came her daughter.
Ivanka and Chelsea were once known as friends.
In one or two decades they might make amends.
But each was superb at her parent's convention,
Giving Clinton and Trump a more human dimension.
Then at last it was Hillary's time to appear;
She held onto Chelsea while Bill shed a tear.
A wrinkle-free forehead, from Botox, I'd guess—
Our political women can't look like a mess.
She was glowing, composed, resplendent in white,
And she rose to the challenge; tonight was her night.
The audience chanted that "love will trump hate,"
And Clinton agreed that our bonds make us great.
We are stronger together, a village is needed,
Else the hardships we face will continue unheeded.
Our forefathers fought a unique revolution
So we could enjoy a secure constitution.

She was gallant to Sanders and gave him her thanks,
And she vowed that together they'd fight for his planks.
Campaigns are poetic, but governing's prose—
Though her speech wasn't lyric, her words soared and rose.
Most viewers agreed she was warm, strong, and steady;
She showed that for POTUS, she's eager and ready.

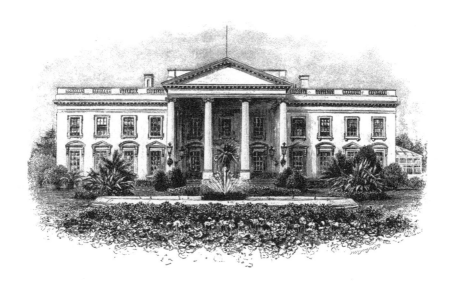

Hillary Clinton accepted the Democratic nomination for president on July 28, 2016.

TransDemocrats

August 3, 2016

Republicans for Clinton—
The list is getting long.
Trump's flare-up with the Khans
Convinced them that he's wrong.
Wrong character, wrong tone,
A serial defrauder,
A spiteful, thin-skinned bully,
A GOP marauder.
But Democrats for Trump?
I've yet to see a list.
I've looked at length online—
Does such a thing exist?
Meg Whitman's now for Clinton.
A Jeb aide followed suit,
A Christie aide did also.
Don't hold your breath for Newt.

▶ Several Republican donors and political professionals announced their support for Clinton because of Trump's continuously outrageous behavior, including his derision of the parents of Army Captain Humayun Khan, a heroic Muslim-American soldier killed in Iraq.

Olympic Campaigns

August 9, 2016

On the economy, Trump made a speech.
I'd rather watch volleyball played on a beach.
Some in his party believe he's a fool.
Hush, there goes Phelps again, owning the pool.
Clinton announced a new job-growing scheme.
I'd rather see Aly cavort on the beam.
Who's the next lawmaker Trump won't endorse?
Hush, there are Russian girls vaulting the horse.
Trump doesn't seem to think Russia's a menace.
I heard Andy Murray's in Rio for tennis.
Much of our country finds Clinton conniving.
I'm spellbound by China's incredible diving.
What do you think about China and trade?
Can anyone tell me how judo is played?
How many emails has Clinton concealed?
Oh, boy, I can't wait till they show track and field!
I'm very dismayed at your shallow reaction.
I care, but find Rio a welcome distraction!

▶ Trump gave a major economic-policy speech on August 8, after a week of declining poll numbers and damaging headlines on several fronts—including his continued disparagement of the parents of a fallen Muslim-American soldier and his initial refusal to endorse Congressman Paul Ryan and Senator John McCain in their re-election campaigns. The speech—which covered taxes, trade, China, and more—was an attempt to show his serious side and launch a turnaround, but many Americans found a pleasant diversion in the Olympics, held August 5–21 in Rio de Janeiro.

Trumpet! (or Campaign Disdain)

August 16, 2016

Improbable candidate Trump is imploding.
Support from beyond Donald's base is eroding.
He says what he wants when in front of a crowd;
What others just think, Donald bellows out loud.
There's always a new and bizarre proclamation
That startles an already cynical nation.
He attacked a sad couple who lost a brave son
And hinted that Clinton could fall by a gun.
He wink-winked to Second Amendment fanatics
To heighten a rally's unruly dramatics.
He's clearly addicted to cheers from the crowd—
That's why he continues, unleashed and unbowed.
His daughter Ivanka has tried to restrain him.
His backers are doing their best to explain him.
Nude shots of his wife were exposed in the *Post*—
No worries, they gave him a new chance to boast.
He thinks that his "skill" with the world's top beauties
Equips him for global diplomacy duties.
When he claimed that Obama's a founder of ISIS,
The GOP mainstream remained in a crisis:
Do they hang on with Donald or find a new man?
Can election-law experts devise a new plan?
With Clinton now courting Mitt Romney's old base,
And giving his voters a cautious embrace,
Will they stay with their party to keep it afloat
Or throw up their hands and give Clinton their vote?
When Trump sees his poll numbers swerve to the south,
He still cannot govern what spews from his mouth,
So how can he govern a vigorous nation
Without risking worldwide vilification?

▶ Trump's campaign continued its downward path in mid-August, after several blunders and outrageous statements. For example, at a raucous rally on August 9, he suggested that "Second Amendment people" could take matters into their own hands if Clinton, as president, appointed judges who favored stricter gun safety measures. The next day, he called President Obama the "founder of ISIS," and didn't back down when questioned by a conservative radio show host. On August 17, the day after this poem was written, Trump hired Steve Bannon, chairman of the far-right site Breitbart News, for the campaign's chief executive officer, in an attempt to right the ship.

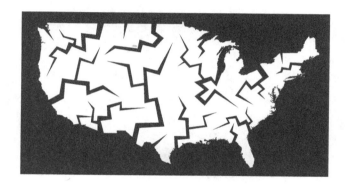

Foundation Frustration

August 25, 2016

The Clinton Foundation has worldwide ties.
Some say its good work obscures favors and lies,
Yet others say no, its objective is weighty,
Fighting hunger and illness from Rwanda to Haiti.
But what if some folks who made mega donations
Harbor "quid pro quo" wishes and high expectations?
The Saudis, said Trump, gave a massive amount
But even if Trump doesn't know how to count,
Donations from sexist, repressive regimes
Are at odds with the Clinton Foundation's main themes—
Like empowering girls to lead full active lives,
Which may *not* be what donors prefer for their wives.
If they're close to the Saudis, akin to the Bushes,
Would they favor agendas a Saudi prince pushes?
No, Hillary has much more honor than that;
She'd be highly unlikely to go "tit for tat."
But appearances count, and thus the foundation
Should surely consider a recalibration.
Appointing a non-Clinton head if she wins
Will deter speculation of quid-pro-quo sins.
Yet a Clinton M.O. lurks that's hard to dispel:
When they strive to do GOOD, they always do WELL!
(As in policies GOOD for the poor and for health,
And WELL for themselves, as in power and wealth.)

▶ In late August, the Associated Press reported that many private citizens who met with
Clinton when she was Secretary of State donated to the Clinton Foundation. Trump
pounced on the report to attack her, claiming that the foundation was a pay-to-play
scheme in which Hillary and Bill Clinton traded government access for donations.
Hillary Clinton's campaign denounced the report, maintaining that its methodol-
ogy was flawed. The campaign noted that as Secretary of State, she met with thousands of people around the world, and a very small number of them donated to

the foundation. Although some political observers thought the foundation's proce-dures might present ethical concerns, others enumerated its many achievements, such as lowering the price of HIV/AIDS medication in Africa and educating women and girls. Moreover, even if the optics were bad, there was no evidence that official favors were granted in exchange for donations. Ironically, Trump chaired a much smaller namesake foundation—The Donald J. Trump Foundation—that reportedly used foundation funds to buy a six-foot-tall portrait of himself and to benefit his for-profit endeavors.

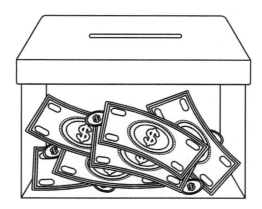

Mr. Weiner's Misdemeanor

August 31, 2016

Anthony Weiner lived up to his name,
An addled text addict—has he no shame?
Though most knew that Weiner was not a great catch,
With Huma he made an improbable match.
But Huma was more or less always away;
She traipsed after Hillary, day after day,
As a trusted advisor and well-traveled aide,
While her husband sat home, texted photos, and strayed.
And even when trying a comeback as mayor,
He kept up his texting, a chronic betrayer.
You'd think that while running for high public office
He'd show some control and become extra cautious
But his cravings and unconscious need to be caught
Soon prevailed over prudence and rational thought.
Now Trump says that Weiner's uncouth immaturity
Might harm and imperil our nation's security.
Yes, Donald said Carlos might put us in Danger
(And could this election become any stranger?).
We know Hillary's bond with poor Huma is strong
And perhaps there's good reason the two get along:
Yes, Hillary understands mortification—
A husband's misdeeds aired in front of the nation.
And smiling in public through each allegation
While stewing in silence with mounting frustration.
Gallant Huma stayed put in the face of each scandal
But at last he was more than she wanted to handle
So Huma left Weiner; she's better alone,
But will he continue to sext on his phone?
His promising future was ruined years ago
But they have a small child who one day will know
That his father's misdeeds made his mother's heart sink,
So Anthony Weiner, please go to a shrink!

► At the end of August 2016, former U.S. Congressman Anthony Weiner (D-NY) was caught "sexting," not for the first time. The episode made national headlines, in part because Weiner's wife was Huma Abedin, Hillary Clinton's longtime aide. Weiner had resigned from Congress in 2011 in the wake of his first sexting scandal. In 2013, while attempting a run for mayor of New York City, he was embroiled in a second sexting episode, this time using the alias "Carlos Danger." The day after the 2016 scandal emerged, Abedin, who was then vice chair of Clinton's campaign, announced that she was leaving Weiner.

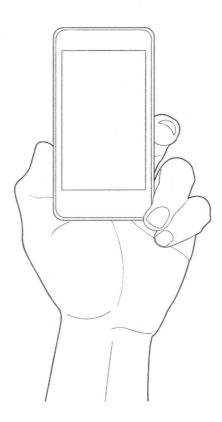

News Roundup: Integrity and Health

September 20, 2016

He stiffed contractors, architects, builders, and others.
His sham of a school swindled poor single mothers
And veterans, widows, and unemployed dreamers
Who lost all their savings to Trump and his schemers.
U.S. banks will not touch him; he doesn't repay.
His investors are foreign; they may want their say,
Posing conflicts that might be a threat to our nation,
More harmful than risks from the Clinton Foundation.
But Hillary had an unfortunate week,
Which pulled down her poll numbers, far from their peak.
She defined Donald's fans with deplorable phrasing
That many agreed with but still found amazing—
You *don't* cut down *voters*; you slam your opponents!
She's sadly still dense on campaigning's components.
She failed to learn lessons from Romney's descent,
With his quip that rebuked forty-seven percent.
On September 11th her knees gave and buckled,
"Which is *proof* she's not well," Donald's voters all chuckled.
And a doctor's weird letter, in Trump's boasting style,
Said that Donald's quite healthy, except for that bile
That spews from his lips now instead of his liver,
A sign of a sickness that *should* make you *shiver*!

▶ Trump's base turned a blind eye to his many transgressions—including his failure to pay contractors and his promotion of a fraudulent "university." His refusal to release his tax returns raised questions about his possible business entanglements with foreign entities, but his fans didn't care. As Trump once said, he could shoot someone on Fifth Avenue without losing supporters. Clinton was not so lucky; she stumbled in September, figuratively and literally, and her poll numbers dropped. At a campaign gala on September 9, she said half of Trump's supporters could be put into "a basket of deplorables," a characterization easy for Republicans to condemn. Then, while leaving a 9/11 memorial service, her knees buckled and her Secret Service detail swiftly helped her into a waiting van. Cameras, however, caught her near-fall, and Republicans questioned her health and strength. Earlier, Trump's doctor had attested to Trump's good health in a letter filled with Donald-style hyperbole that did not seem to be written by a medical professional (the candidate, for example, had "astonishingly excellent" lab results and would be the "healthiest individual ever elected to the presidency").

Debate, Round One

September 27, 2016

Democrats breathed a huge sigh of relief:
Hillary shone; Donald lied through his teeth.
Clinton was eloquent, solid, and strong;
Donald meandered and went on too long.
The host showed restraint and at times disappeared,
And Trump did less damage than Democrats feared.
Hillary's health seemed 100 percent;
Donald was sniffling throughout the event.
Substance was slight but they did discuss trade—
Donald was trying but rambled and strayed.
If Trump paid no taxes, he said he was "smart,"
Which shows he won't have our best interests at heart.
He's proud he saw profit with housing in crisis,
And weirdly said Hill spent her life fighting ISIS.
Debates might make reference to Mitchell McConnell
But why would Trump talk about Rosie O'Donnell?
Trump was defensive but didn't stoop too low;
Next time, he warned us, that's where he might go.

▶ September 26 marked the first presidential debate between Trump and Clinton, with NBC anchor Lester Holt moderating. The antagonism between the two candidates was palpable. Democrats fretted beforehand; they were afraid Trump would lash into her unmercifully, as he had done with his Republican rivals. But Clinton was clear, strong, and well prepared, while Trump was erratic and unfocused, especially toward the end of the evening. Insults and accusations outnumbered policy points. Clinton reminded viewers that Trump had "rooted for the housing crisis" because it gave him opportunities to make money. Trump criticized Clinton for supporting free trade agreements that, he claimed, have cost Americans jobs. Clinton disparaged Trump for failing to release his tax returns, noting that when a set of his returns became public years ago, they revealed that he had paid no income tax. "That makes me smart," he retorted. Clinton criticized Trump for his demeaning attitude toward women. To defend himself, Trump claimed that most of his insults had been directed at comedian Rosie O'Donnell, with whom he had feuded on and off for a decade, and "everybody would agree that she deserves it." Trump also noted that he had planned to say "something extremely rough" about Bill Clinton and his extramarital affairs, but decided against it because the Clintons' daughter, Chelsea, was in the audience.

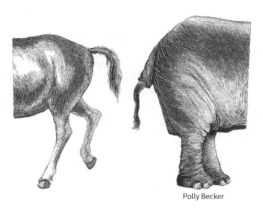

Polly Becker

Wary of Gary

September 29, 2016

"Who's your favorite foreign leader, anywhere at all?"
"Maybe, like, well, umm ...," Gary Johnson tried to stall.
"You gotta do this, Governor, to show you've got the stuff.
If you wanna be our president, this question isn't tough."
"Uh, the Mexican who, earlier, before the current guy...."
Sympathetic people might say that's a decent try
But Gary in that interview was having mental blocks—
His running mate Bill Weld assisted, stating "Vincente Fox."
Gary ran New Mexico with brazen budget cuts
But on non-domestic matters Gary clearly is a klutz—
Aleppo is in Syria and Paris is in France—
Gary should have studied foreign nations in advance.
Legalizing pot may make you popular with kids
But otherwise, dear Gary, your campaign is on the skids
So please don't try to enter any Clinton-Trump debate—
It's clear that being president is nowhere in your fate.

▶ Former New Mexico Governor Gary Johnson, known for favoring limited government
and legalization of marijuana, decided to run for president on the Libertarian ticket.
Former Massachusetts Governor William Weld, a moderate Republican, was his running mate. (Even so, Weld seemed to favor Clinton, whom he had known since they
worked together on the Watergate impeachment inquiry in the 1970s.) Johnson did
not meet the threshold of support to participate in the presidential debates, but political commentator Chris Matthews interviewed the pair on MSNBC. He asked Johnson to name his "favorite foreign leader," but Johnson couldn't think of one. Less
than two weeks earlier, Johnson had flubbed another interview; he was unfamiliar
with Aleppo, the Syrian city torn by civil war and a refugee crisis.

Pensive

October 5, 2016

Tim Kaine came out swinging with gusto and vigor.
Mike Pence was controlled but he lied with a snigger.
Yes, Kaine interrupted but Pence did it too
And blew past the host just as men often do.
When discussing their faith, they both seemed to relax—
That's an easier topic than Donald and tax!
Tim's down-to-earth charm, alas, failed to come through;
His role as attacker was still somewhat new.
He rose fairly often to Clinton's defense
And criticized Trump to provoke and goad Pence,
But Pence did not take up the bait; he stayed cool.
In private perhaps he thinks Donald's a fool.
He agreed nonetheless to become Donald's Veep
As a shortcut for reaching the top of the heap—
He'll garner the nationwide name recognition
That's needed to fuel a much larger ambition,
So don't be surprised if in four short years hence
The GOP ticket on top features Pence!

▶ On October 4, 2016, the vice presidential candidates, Senator Tim Kaine of Virginia and Governor Mike Pence of Indiana, held their only debate, with Elaine Quijano of CBS News as moderator. It was more fiery than expected. Kaine, normally congenial and personable, played the role of attack dog, assailing Trump for his failure to release his tax returns and other issues. After strong showings in early September, Trump was struggling in the polls—a series of outbursts had once again raised questions about his temperament and fitness for office. Pence was calm and reassuring, probably in an effort to appeal to voters concerned about Trump's disposition. Even so, Pence struggled to defend some of Trump's controversial statements and even denied that Trump had made a few of them. Both VP candidates are known for their strong faith, and one of the debate's more authentic moments came when the moderator asked about the relationship between their religion and their policy positions.

Seldom Sorry

October 8, 2016

When putting an end to his birther campaign,
"The Donald" said Clinton's the one we should blame.
Can't Trump ever issue a simple apology?
He said he regretted the coarse terminology
That was caught on a tape from a decade ago
On a bus on the way to a Hollywood show,
But again he brought Hillary into the fray
By declaring that when her dear husband would stray
She would "bully, attack and then shame" each accuser,
And excuse her cad husband, a "woman abuser."
And although Trump admitted his language was crude,
He said Bill is "far worse" and yes, even more lewd.
The internet's buzzing; this clickbait is easy—
The public adores any scoop that is sleazy!
McConnell and Ryan were more than appalled
While Hillary's team was engrossed and enthralled.
And some say that Trump now should get the hell out—
The GOP brass fear a down-ticket rout.

▶ October 7, a shockwave hit the news: a hot-mic video recording from the "Access Hollywood" TV show in 2005, leaked to the *Washington Post*, showed Trump bragging about kissing, groping, and attempting to have sex with women. "When you're a star," he said, "they let you do it. You can do anything.... Grab them by the pussy." Later that day, Trump apologized in a short video statement. He added, however, that his "foolish" words were a far cry from the *actions* of Bill Clinton, whom he accused of abusing women, and Hillary Clinton, who, in Trump's words, "bullied, attacked, shamed, and intimidated [Bill's] victims." This was not the first time Trump had shifted the blame and negative focus to Hillary Clinton. In mid-September, when he finally withdrew his "birther" allegations and acknowledged that President Obama was born in the U.S., Trump claimed that doubts about Obama's birthplace had originated with Hillary Clinton in her 2008 primary campaign against Obama.

Dear Donald Re: Debate Number Two

October 11, 2016

You prowled on the stage like a strange hulking bear.
Your comportment was just as bizarre as your hair.
You lied and you seethed and you called her the devil.
You sunk to a boorish, unstatesmanlike level.
You blamed her for ISIS, the tax code, and Syria,
As "proved" by your specious and hollow criteria.
You played to your base and they liked what they saw:
A swaggering Donald whose rage did not thaw.
They admired your self-assured, blustering tone.
They agreed when you said that her heart's made of stone.
In tin-pot republics and fascist regimes
A dictator jails an opponent who seems
To threaten his status as head of the state,
But Donald, you know why America's GREAT?
Our leaders don't say that, not even if kidding;
Our judges don't follow a president's bidding.
We have laws and procedures designed to be fair
And safeguards of which you seem quite unaware.
Some thought you did well in the second debate,
But the bar's set so low that we sometimes equate
A person who's famous and forceful and confident
With one who is strong, well-informed, and yes, competent.

▶ The second Trump–Clinton debate, moderated by Martha Raddatz of ABC and Anderson Cooper of CNN, was held two days after the release of the "Access Hollywood" videotape. Trump's campaign was suffering, and several notable Republicans had publicly abandoned him. To deflect from the vulgarity of the tape, the Trump campaign hosted, less than two hours before the debate, a surprise "press conference" featuring a group of women who had accused Bill Clinton of sexual assault. At the debate itself, the hostility between the two candidates was visible from the outset: they broke protocol by declining to shake hands. Trump attacked Clinton relentlessly, blaming her for a host of ills. He said she would "be in jail" if he were president, and he even referred to her as "the devil." His combative performance may have appealed to his base, but it didn't help with mainstream voters. His demeanor was odd and unnerving—he loomed behind Clinton, scowling at times when she spoke. It wasn't her best debate performance, but she was calm and poised while Trump prowled behind her.

Irony: No More Pussyfooting for Many Voters

October 18, 2016

Yes, finally, women are turning to Hillary!
They've a pent-up desire to punish and pillory
A man who reminds them of years of frustration,
But Hillary *isn't* their chief inspiration.
Yes, women came forward, suddenly bold—
Trump opened the floodgates to stories untold:
That time in your early and innocent teens
When the "nice boy" next door thrust his hand down your jeans,
That time when your date thought that starting to flirt
Gave him license to shove his big paws down your shirt,
That time at the doctor's when something quite hard
Rubbed your hip while you lay there, prone and off guard,
That time when the man in the nice suit and tie
Shook your hand with respect ... but then stroked your thigh,
That time when the Ivy League man oozing class
Called a feminist writer a nice piece of ass....
Yes, Trump the lewd braggart got women to rally
And moved undecideds to Hillary's tally.

▶ Trump's crude banter on the "Access Hollywood" videotape prompted many women to reveal, often for the first time, their own experiences with sexual assault. The *New York Times* called the video "a rallying cry for survivors of sexual assault [and] harassment," with "multitudes of women [coming] forward to share their stories." A Twitter query from a social media personality—"Women: tweet me your first assaults"—drew more than a million responses in a single evening. Some political observers thought the video would be lethal to Trump's campaign. Clinton had had trouble reaching female voters—especially younger women—but many decided to vote for her after witnessing Trump's coarse bragging. Even so, the video—"old news" by November—did not drive female voters away from Trump as much as the Clinton campaign had anticipated. (Almost a year later, the exposure of Harvey Weinstein's behavior stirred an even greater public outcry and prompted more women to come forward with accounts of sexual harassment and assault.)

Oh, What a Night!

October 20, 2016

Yes, many were dreading the final debate—
Would Trump pull new tricks, out of malice and hate?
The last time, he gathered a group of Bill's gals
So why not invite more embarrassing pals—
A shapely young intern, sporting a thong?
An ersatz Obama, smoking a bong?
A ghoulish Vince Foster, back from the dead?
Or maybe Obama's half-brother instead?
Oh, Hillary, yes, "they go low, we go high,"
But please, can't you give "going low" a nice try?
The issues are dreary—America's hoping
For easier topics, like kissing and groping!
Hooray, you alluded to Jessica Leeds,
The target of Donald's lewd mid-air misdeeds,
And others he thought he could fondle or ogle
Simply because he's a billionaire mogul.
"The Florida killer and Trump are from Queens!"
Hooray, that was low; I'm not sure what it means.
Donald at first seemed composed and coherent—
He made it quite clear he's a pro-gun adherent
But on Roe versus Wade, Donald wasn't as clear
Till his graphic descriptions made right-wingers cheer.
Chris Wallace at first was commanding and tough
But his clout and control soon were *not* quite enough.
As the evening wore on, Donald blathered and rambled,
He often digressed, and his phrases were scrambled.
When Wallace asked Trump, if he lost in the race,
In a rather disturbing display of disgrace,
Trump implied he would question the people's selection
And allege it's a rigged and a crooked election.
"A democracy-dwelling, well-balanced adult
As a rule will accept an election result,"

The pundits responded and censured and wailed.
His defenders, like Conway, evaded and flailed.
But CNN *scored* the big hit of the night,
When two of its pundits engaged in a fight—
Van Jones, who's a self-described stats-and-facts nerd,
Nonetheless said, "You can't *polish* this *turd*!"

▶ Chris Wallace of Fox News moderated the third and final debate. Trump pulled another "stunt," inviting President Barack Obama's Kenyan-born half-brother, who
had endorsed Trump. The candidate showed his mean-spiritedness in other ways,
at one point calling Clinton "a nasty woman." Although Michelle Obama, at the Democratic National Convention, had famously said, "When they go low, we go high,"
Clinton decided to "go low" this time. For example, she mentioned Jessica Leeds,
a woman who said Trump had groped her "like an octopus" on an airplane many
years ago. Clinton also brought up the gunman who had murdered 49 people in Orlando, oddly noting that he, like Trump, was from Queens. The candidates sparred
over substance, too, chiefly on the Second Amendment and abortion rights. Trump
had hoped to recover from a difficult three weeks, with his poll numbers in decline
since early October. At first, he seemed to be having a good night, but he gradually
fell apart, with incoherent answers and snorts. The most alarming part of the debate was Trump's refusal to commit to accepting the election results; he thought the
election could be rigged against him. Wallace challenged Trump: "But, sir, ... one of
the prides of this country is the peaceful transition of power.... [T]he loser concedes
to the winner." In a contentious exchange after the debate, CNN commentator Van
Jones challenged his colleague Kayleigh McEnany when she tried to spin Trump's
declaration about the election results. Jones countered that there was no way to
gloss over it: "This is a very sad night for this country. You can't polish this turd." He
added that Trump's refusal to respect "the process and the outcome" demonstrated
an "appalling lack of patriotism."

Humiliated Huma and Her Homemade Hell

October 31, 2016

Hillary's emails will not go away!
Anthony Weiner is back in the fray!
Sending his dick-pics to underage females
Opened the door to his harried wife's emails.
The FBI ordered a hazmat-gear shipment
To handle his iPad and other equipment.
Sharing a laptop with weird husband Weiner,
Huma sent emails but should've foreseen her
Marriage to Tony would not turn out well.
But *was* it too much of a stretch to foretell
That his carnal and crass electronic advances
Could dash or derail her dear Hillary's chances?

▶ On October 28, eleven days before the election, FBI Director James Comey disclosed that the bureau had discovered potential new evidence relating to Clinton's use of a private email server. During an unrelated investigation into former U.S. Congressman Anthony Weiner's sexually explicit text messages to an underage girl, agents seized a computer that Weiner shared with his wife, Huma Abedin, Clinton's longtime aide. The FBI was reviewing emails found on the shared computer. The Justice Department had advised Comey to delay the disclosure until after the emails had been reviewed, even if that process lasted beyond the election. Not surprisingly, Comey's disclosure was front-page news and a cable-TV sensation. Two days before the election, Comey announced that the emails had *not* turned up anything new; they were mostly personal and duplicates of what had already been seen. But the impact of his disclosure and its intense media coverage would not recede.

Election Obsession

November 3, 2016

I can't relax, I'm glued online,
I fixate on the latest sign
That Donald may be gaining ground,
Or Clinton may not come around.
The emails, groping, talk of rape—
They make me want to hit "escape!"
A stranger tells me what to think
On Facebook with a tempting link.
My daily fix of TV news
Stars pundits with competing views.
Oh, Rachel, Anderson, or Don,
Please let me know what's going on!
I listen closely, then I sigh,
'Cause they know little more than I.
But *still* I watch them, just in case,
There's breaking news, a new disgrace,
A pivot in this crazy race,
A raucous call to Donald's base,
Another Weiner fall from grace,
An FBI man out of place,
Or tantalizing public peek
At emails from a hacker's leak.
I cannot bear to miss a beat,
A sign of promise or defeat.
My sips of pinot noir at night
Are not enough to quell my fright.
Oh, Slate, Salon, oh, CNN,
Can someone somewhere tell me when
My normal need for nightly news
Became a craze I can't defuse?
My home's a mess, my work is late,
Yet still I never hesitate

To look online for one more poll,
But HELP, I haven't got control....
Just "one more poll" turns into more
And pretty soon my eyes are sore
And afternoon has turned to night
And still there's not an end in sight.
But YES, there IS: Election Day!
My nerves and common sense will fray.
Oh, will I sob or will I gloat....
I hope I don't forget to vote!

▶ Many people suffered from intense anxiety in the days before the 2016 presidential election. The campaigns leading up to it were perhaps the most contentious, and definitely the most tawdry, in recent U.S. history. Although every presidential election brings some level of angst, the fight between Clinton and Trump seemed to take a greater toll.

PART THREE

The Election and Its Immediate Aftermath

A November Surprise

Nearly every poll for months, right up to Election Day, predicted a huge victory for Clinton. But as the election results came in, her supporters grew baffled, then panicky and unnerved, as Trump emerged the victor. Headlines announced the unexpected win with words like "stunning" and "shocker." Clinton's victory in the popular vote was cold comfort.

November 2016

Sunday	Monday	Tuesday	Wednesday	Thursday	Friday	Saturday
		1	2	3	4	5
6	7	✔ 8	9	10	11	12
13	14	15	16	17	18	19
20	21	22	23	24	25	26
27	28	29	30			

OCTOBER 2016   DECEMBER 2016

Stunning and Cunning

November 9, 2016

How could polling be so wrong
And not predict that Trump was strong?!
Yes, Trump's the victor, loud and clear,
And Clinton's fans convulsed with fear.
Michigan was neck and neck,
Pennsylvania, what the heck!?
"A stunning upset!" shrieked the news
As Clinton's cohorts sang the blues.
The global finance markets crashed
As Clinton's lofty hopes were dashed.
Some said Comey bore the blame
Or can't we yet elect a dame?
Or maybe blame the frantic news,
Which values numbers, clicks, and views,
Or right-wing groups that aim to strip
The Voting Rights Act of its grip.
On CNN, Van Jones maintained
An ugly "whitelash" was unchained,
A backlash to our first black POTUS,
Putting Democrats on notice—
"This country's changing much too fast
And we prefer our rosy past,"
A past that Donald swore he missed,
A past that never did exist.
His win surprised the anxious world,
So *now* get *set* for Trump, *unfurled*.

▶ Polls had predicted that Clinton would win in the Electoral College and the key battle-
ground states she ended up losing—Michigan, Pennsylvania, and Wisconsin (reliably
Democratic states in the last six presidential elections, and in Wisconsin's case, the
last seven). Commentators wondered how polling experts could make such a co-
lossal mistake. "Pollsters flubbed the 2016 presidential election in seismic fashion,"

declared *USA Today*. Global financial markets dropped overnight (when this poem was written) amid fears of trade turmoil and policy uncertainty under Trump. (In the U.S., stock markets initially fell on the day after the election, but rose by midday and ended up soaring.) After Trump's victory, Clinton and others maintained that Comey's disclosure about possible new emails—a mere 11 days before the election—was a key factor in her loss. Later, statistics expert Nate Silver of fivethirtyeight.com calculated that the impact of Comey's disclosure was probably enough to change the Electoral College result.

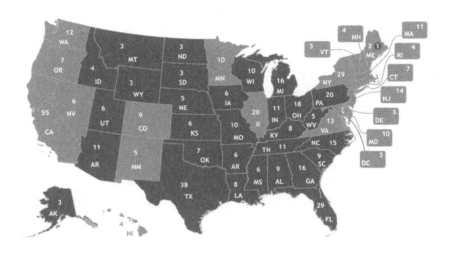

Election Reflection: What's a Liberal to Do?

November 13, 2016

Pretend it never happened and escape from real life.
  No, demonstrate with placards and find unity in strife!
Watch mysteries and sci-fi and indulge in Netflix dramas.
  Get active; save the legacy that proudly is Obama's!
Ignore the news forever and read only arts and sports.
  No, work to keep Scalia-clones from clogging up the courts!
Indulge in carbs and candy and drink a lot of wine.
  No, plan for an impeachment and demand that Trump resign!
But that would bring us Pence whose hard-right views will never thaw.
  Then protest and prevent those views from jelling into law!
I'll fantasize a move, perhaps to Canada or Sweden.
  No, stay and work for progress that we know we can succeed in!
I'll learn obscure statistics as a baseball-nut obsessive.
  That's selfish and indulgent for a person who's progressive.
Or go for days on end without a glance at any screen.
  No, follow online posts to see what trendlines you can glean.
Or pray that Trump as president's not Trump the crazed campaigner.
  I doubt he'll change; at root, he's just a B-grade entertainer.
Ivanka, once a Democrat, might calm his callous stances.
  Your optimism's flawed; your little pipedream has no chances.
But maybe he'll adjust his views on healthcare and the wall.
  I doubt that once in office he'll be president for all.
I hope he'll learn before too long to weigh opposing voices.
  For America's salvation he may have no other choices.
And maybe he'll denounce the hate that fueled his mad campaign.
  *And **keep** our country **great** by acting civil and humane!*

▶ Trump's victory astounded and worried Democrats. Some were in denial and wanted to escape reality; others vowed to become politically active to resist Trump's polices. Many felt a mix of the two reactions.

Presidential Predilections: His Favorite Things

December 2, 2016

Penthouses, power, and plutocrat nations,
Rallies with cheering and standing ovations,
Big brassy buildings and homes fit for kings,
These are a few of his favorite things.

Girls in low necklines and curve-hugging dresses,
Towering heels and long flowing tresses,
Diamonds that dazzle and clothing that clings,
These are a few of his favorite things.

Conflicts and chaos and looming corruption,
Falsehoods and flare-ups, a Twitter eruption,
Favors for fawners that come with tight strings,
These are a few of his favorite things.

When the press bites, when the *Times* stings,
When he's feeling mad,
He'll simply remember his favorite things,
And then he won't feel so bad.

"Hamilton," flag burning, SNL sketches—
When he's upset he bites back and he kvetches.
Wait till he sees what his new office brings....
Bet you they won't be his favorite things!

Putty for Putin and fodder for Bannon,
Trump is a thin-skinned, reactive loose cannon.
They might have sway in his policy swings—
Could be he's one of their favorite things.

▶ Apologies—and credit—go to Rodgers and Hammerstein for this song parody.

Trump's Cabinet of Curiosities: Expertise, Please!

December 10, 2016
Updated January 26, 2017,
and October 1, 2017

Polly Becker

Intro

For chicken coop security
He'd choose a crafty fox.
For national posterity
He's cast a baleful pox:

Michael Flynn
(National Security Advisor)

The person who may guide us
Through a global terror threat
Retweets fake news that's senseless,
Which he always fails to vet.

Betsy DeVos (Secretary of Education)

The pick for education
Perhaps is not a fool
But neither has she set a toe
Inside a public school.

Ben Carson (Secretary of Housing and Urban Development)

The man who may lead HUD
Is anti-public housing.
"Poverty's a state of mind"
Is what he's been espousing.

Andrew Puzder (Secretary of Labor)

The nominee for Labor
Thinks workers waste time eating.
He'd rather hire robots
To ensure that we're competing.

Nikki Haley (Ambassador to the United Nations)
With parents born abroad,
The choice for U.N. rep
Lacks other foreign know-how—
She'd better start to prep!

Scott Pruitt (Head of the Environmental Protection Agency)
The pick for EPA
Says "Climate change? No dice!"
He likes Big Oil's money
And ignores the melting ice.

Ryan Zinke (Secretary of the Interior)
The nominee entrusted
To protect our public land
Might offer coal and logging
Permission to expand.

Linda McMahon (Head of the Small Business Administration)
Pro wrestling is a world
With rules that are its own.
Kaboom, the new small business head
Could soon be overthrown!

Rick Perry (Secretary of Energy)
If you don't respect
And cannot recollect
The group you may direct,
There's a major disconnect!

Rex Tillerson (Secretary of State)
A pal of Putin's plutocrats
Might be our rep abroad.
His email system needs to have
Encryption that's unflawed!

Tom Price (Secretary of Health and Human Services)

He gambled with his healthcare stocks,
Accumulating wealth.
He'd trade away our Medicaid
And gamble with our health.

Steven Mnuchin (Secretary of the Treasury)

A foreclosure king for Treasury
Won't help to drain the swamp.
For him the Great Recession was
A moneymaking romp.

Jeff Sessions (Attorney General)

His record is abysmal
On civil rights and race.
The nominee for new A.G.:
A national disgrace.

▶ By December 10, Trump had announced most of the candidates for his Cabinet and other key posts. All seemed uniquely unqualified for their possible new roles. Most disagreed with the missions of the very agencies they had been tapped to run. For example, Scott Pruitt, the nominee for the Environmental Protection Agency (EPA), had filed lawsuits against the agency when he was Attorney General of Oklahoma, and had even called for its elimination. Secretary of Education nominee Betsy DeVos had no experience working with public schools and scant knowledge of education policy and concepts. Michael Flynn, the proposed National Security Advisor (who later was forced to resign), had tweeted fake news, conspiracy theories, and dubious claims about the Clintons. Former Texas Governor Rick Perry, nominated to head the Department of Energy, once proclaimed that he wanted to abolish it (although he couldn't recall its name at the time). Tom Price, the pick for Health and Human Services, wanted to dismantle some of its programs. He had made money in healthcare stocks while serving as a congressman involved in healthcare policy. (He resigned in September 2017 amid controversy over his use of taxpayer-funded private planes.) Andrew Pudzer, the nominee for Secretary of Labor (he later withdrew), had discussed replacing fast-food workers with robots; the latter, he noted, never take vacations and don't sue for discrimination.

Clueless on Lewis

January 16, 2017

He risked his life for civil rights,
And joined in key reformist fights
In Alabama, then the House,
But now, a presidential louse,
On Twitter, in a senseless squawk,
Claims Lewis just is "talk talk talk."
In '65 when John was beaten
And forced to take a back-end seat in
Buses in some Southern states,
Trump was going out on dates,
And playing squash and having fun,
Oblivious to *any*one
Whose social life was drab or dull.
And that's when troopers bashed John's skull.
So, Trump, you *know* what makes us GREAT?
We're *free* to speak and demonstrate,
And criticize a politician.
A tyrant sees that as sedition.
Your thin-skinned disrespect for Lewis
Proves again you're cruel and clueless.

▶ The president-elect sneered at Congressman John Lewis, the civil rights icon, on the eve of Martin Luther King Jr. Day weekend. Lewis had decided to skip the inauguration, and he questioned Trump's legitimacy as president because of Russia's interference in the election. In retaliation, Trump tweeted that Lewis was "All talk, talk, talk—no action or results. Sad." Lewis, however, was never "just talk"; he truly walked the walk. For example, in 1965, he was beaten and almost killed by police in Selma, Alabama, when he marched for civil rights alongside Martin Luther King Jr. Trump seemed not to know Lewis's background, just as later, during a Black History Month event, Trump seemed to believe that Frederick Douglass—the 19th century abolitionist and writer who was once a slave—was a current leader.

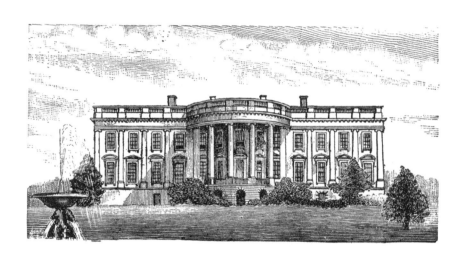

ACKNOWLEDGMENTS

Writing poems throughout the tempestuous campaign season was cathartic for me, but I didn't do it alone. I thank everyone who gave me feedback along the way, including my sister, Amy Fine Collins, and my friends Marilyn Mufson and Emily Soltanoff. Emily also designed the front cover. In addition, I thank my eagle-eyed friend Marie Lefton, whose detailed comments seemed to pinpoint every word, phrase, or innuendo that had concerned me. I am especially grateful to my mother, Elsa Honig Fine, whose editing, proofreading, and observations were indispensable.

Sixteen of the poems in this book (some in slightly different versions) appeared online in Cognoscenti, the news and opinion website of WBUR, an NPR station in Boston. I thank Kelly Horan and Frannie Carr Toth, the co-editors of Cognoscenti during the campaign, for their support and encouragement. They specifically requested a couple of poems in light of breaking news. Composing them in time for Cognoscenti's morning screen made me feel like a true "deadline poet."

I am glad that my father introduced me to Cole Porter when I was in junior high school. Listening to Porter's lyrics over and over for decades no doubt influenced my writing.

ABOUT THE AUTHOR

E rika S. Fine is a freelance writer and editor who has been composing light verse for as long as she can remember. A former lawyer and corporate executive, she lives near Boston with too many books and antiques.